Reimagining America: The Project 2025 Manifesto

By James Albright

Disclaimer

The information, analysis, and opinions expressed in this book are the views of the author and are provided for informational purposes only. The content is based on publicly available sources, personal research, and interpretation. While every effort has been made to ensure the accuracy of the information presented, the author does not claim to be an expert on all aspects of *Project 2025* or related policy issues.

This book does not constitute professional advice, legal recommendations, or financial guidance. Readers are encouraged to conduct their own research, consult with qualified professionals, and consider multiple perspectives when forming their opinions about *Project 2025* or any political, legal, or social issues discussed in this text.

The author and publisher disclaim any liability for any loss or damage caused, directly or indirectly, by the information or opinions provided in this book. Any references to specific organizations, policies, or events are purely for illustrative purposes and do not imply endorsement or criticism by the author or publisher.

Chapter 1: Understanding Project 2025

Imagine waking up to a world where the size of the U.S. government has shrunk, conservative values dominate public policy, and federal agencies once bloated with bureaucracy are lean and efficient. This world isn't far-fetched; it's the vision that *Project 2025* seeks to bring to life. Spearheaded by the Heritage Foundation, this ambitious initiative aims to reshape the American government through policies that reflect a conservative ideology. Whether you agree with these policies or not, it's crucial to understand what this initiative represents and how it could fundamentally change the fabric of American governance.

You might wonder, *why now?* Why is there such an urgent push for a massive overhaul of the federal government? The answer lies in what the Heritage Foundation and its partners view as a need to correct what they see as liberal overreach and restore what they describe as true constitutional governance. With an eye on the future, Project 2025 doesn't merely suggest tweaking existing policies—it proposes a radical restructuring of how the federal government operates, how it engages with the American people, and how it affects your daily life.

Overview of Project 2025

At its core, Project 2025 is a blueprint for a conservative U.S. administration, a roadmap to ensure that the next conservative president has the tools, personnel, and policies ready to transform the government on day one. The initiative is not just about policy but also about personnel—ensuring that the right people are in place to carry out its vision of a smaller, more efficient federal government.

The Heritage Foundation, a conservative think tank, is leading this initiative, but they're not alone. Over 100 conservative organizations, including the Family Research Council, American Moment, and the Claremont Institute, have joined forces to make Project 2025 a reality. You may recognize some of these names, but it's essential to understand their collective influence. These organizations, some of which have shaped conservative thought for decades, bring with them a network of policy experts, political strategists, and legal scholars all working in tandem to create a government that aligns with their values.

This initiative's primary goal is to radically reduce the size of the federal government. You've probably heard calls for "small government" before, but Project 2025 takes it a step further. It's not just about cutting taxes or reducing federal spending; it's about reshaping the bureaucracy itself. Imagine thousands of federal employees replaced with individuals handpicked for their conservative credentials, and entire federal agencies either restructured or eliminated. The effects of these changes would ripple through every corner of American life—from the way your local school is funded to how environmental regulations affect your community.

The Heritage Foundation is the mastermind behind Project 2025, but their partners are just as influential. For instance, the Claremont Institute, known for its intellectual and ideological rigor, brings a scholarly approach to conservative governance, while the Family Research Council focuses on aligning policy with Christian conservative values.

What these organizations have in common is a shared vision of an America where federal power is limited, and individual freedoms—particularly religious and economic freedoms—are prioritized. By pooling their resources, these groups aim to create a future conservative administration that is prepared from the moment it takes office. You might not see their work in the headlines every day, but their influence is profound, quietly shaping the policy conversations happening in Washington, D.C.

These organizations are also assembling a vast network of conservative policy experts to populate future federal positions. The idea is that no conservative administration should be caught flat-footed, scrambling to fill key roles. Project 2025's "Presidential Personnel Database" is designed to ensure that a conservative president has immediate access to a pool of ideologically aligned individuals who can step into positions of power and implement conservative policies without hesitation.

Think of it as a government in waiting—a shadow cabinet of sorts, ready to take the reins of power and move the country in a conservative direction. These policy experts are not just focusing on the headline issues of the day, such as immigration and taxes, but also on the nuts and bolts of governance—how federal agencies operate, how regulations are enforced, and how executive orders can be used to bypass what they see as gridlocked legislative processes.

The overarching goals of Project 2025 can be boiled down to three primary objectives: reducing the size of government, restoring conservative policies, and reshaping the federal bureaucracy. Each of these goals is rooted in a desire to return the federal government to what its proponents see as a more constitutionally faithful structure, one that aligns with conservative interpretations of individual liberty, limited government, and free enterprise.

Reducing the Size of Government

Reducing the size of the government is more than just a budget-cutting exercise for Project 2025; it's about fundamentally rethinking the role of the federal government in American life. Proponents argue that the federal government has grown too large and too powerful, infringing on states' rights and individual liberties. You've likely heard calls for "limited government" in conservative circles, but Project 2025 plans to take this a step further by drastically reducing the workforce of federal agencies and reassigning many of their responsibilities to the states.

But what does this mean for you? Imagine fewer federal regulations governing everyday activities, from what your child is taught in school to how your local community manages its environmental resources. While proponents argue that this enhances freedom and state autonomy, critics suggest that it could lead to a patchwork of regulations that vary widely from state to state, potentially causing confusion and inconsistency in areas like healthcare, education, and environmental protection.

Restoring Conservative Policies

Restoring conservative policies is another key pillar of Project 2025. This isn't just about reviving policies from the past but also about introducing new initiatives that reflect conservative values. Immigration reform, tax cuts, deregulation, and stronger executive powers are at the heart of this restoration. You may see this as an opportunity to reintroduce policies that prioritize economic growth, national security, and personal freedoms, but it's essential to also consider the broader implications.

For example, immigration reform under Project 2025 would involve stricter border controls and fewer pathways to citizenship, policies that could have significant impacts on labor markets, community demographics, and international relations. Similarly, tax reforms would prioritize reducing corporate taxes and cutting income taxes for high earners, which could boost economic activity but may also widen the income gap and reduce funding for public services.

Reshaping the Federal Bureaucracy

Perhaps Project 2025's most ambitious goal is its plan to reshape the federal bureaucracy. This involves a significant overhaul of how federal agencies operate and how decisions are made within the executive branch. You might see this as a necessary move to eliminate waste and inefficiency in government, but it also raises concerns about accountability and oversight.

For instance, Project 2025 proposes increasing the power of the executive branch, allowing the president to have more direct control over federal agencies. This would mean that many decisions currently made by career civil servants could instead be made by political appointees who are aligned with the president's agenda. Proponents argue that this would ensure that the government is more responsive to the will of the people, but critics warn that it could undermine the impartiality of federal agencies and concentrate too much power in the hands of the executive.

The Conservative Mandate for Leadership

At the heart of Project 2025 is the *Mandate for Leadership*, a comprehensive guide designed to influence policy in the first 180 days of a future conservative administration. This document isn't just a list of policy proposals; it's a detailed strategy for how a conservative president can reshape the federal government quickly and effectively. The

Mandate for Leadership covers everything from tax reform and deregulation to education policy and environmental regulations.

What makes this document so significant is its focus on immediate action. The first 180 days of any administration are critical, and Project 2025's architects understand that a new conservative president will need to act swiftly to implement their agenda. You can imagine the sense of urgency behind this plan—it's not just about passing legislation but about using executive orders, regulatory changes, and personnel appointments to ensure that conservative policies take root before political opposition has time to mobilize.

Background on the "Mandate for Leadership"

The *Mandate for Leadership* has its roots in the early days of the Reagan administration. Originally published by the Heritage Foundation in 1981, the first *Mandate for Leadership* served as a roadmap for conservative governance and was instrumental in shaping the policies of the Reagan era. Fast forward to today, and Project 2025's version of the *Mandate for Leadership* builds on that legacy, updated for the challenges and opportunities of the 21st century.

For you, the significance of this document lies in its ability to shape not just the policies of a future conservative administration but the structure of government itself. It's not just about conservative values; it's about creating a government that is leaner, more efficient, and more responsive to the president's agenda. Whether you see this as a necessary course correction or a dangerous concentration of power, there's no denying that the *Mandate for Leadership* is poised to have a profound impact on the future of American governance.

In conclusion, Project 2025 represents a bold vision for the future of the U.S. government. It's a vision rooted in conservative principles—smaller government, individual freedoms, and free-market policies—but its reach extends far beyond simple policy proposals. It's about fundamentally reshaping the way the federal government operates, from the personnel who staff it to the policies it enforces. Whether you agree with its goals or not, it's clear that Project 2025 has the potential to transform American governance in ways that will affect every citizen. And as you consider the implications of this ambitious initiative, it's worth asking yourself if you want this for your future.

2025 is a transformative vision for the future of conservative governance in America. Understanding its foundation is essential as you navigate the complexities of modern political policy. This chapter has outlined the goals, key players, and implications of this ambitious plan to reshape the U.S. government and reinstate conservative principles.

By reducing the size of government, Project 2025 promises a leaner, more efficient bureaucracy, one where states take on more power and federal agencies are less intrusive. The initiative goes beyond policies aiming to install a network of ideologically aligned personnel to ensure that conservative principles are not just written into law but also deeply integrated into the everyday functioning of government agencies.

For you, as an American citizen, Project 2025 represents both opportunity and challenge. On one hand, it envisions a government that returns power to the people and aligns with conservative values like free enterprise and individual liberty. On the other hand, its critics argue that the concentration of power in the executive branch and the rollback of certain social programs could disproportionately affect marginalized communities and erode democratic norms.

The *Mandate for Leadership*, central to this vision, is more than just a policy guide—it's a strategic plan to implement these changes swiftly and effectively. The idea that a new conservative administration could make sweeping reforms within the first 180 days highlights the urgency and determination behind this initiative. With the backing of powerful think tanks and policy experts, Project 2025 is poised to leave a lasting mark on the American political landscape.

As you move forward, it's crucial to engage with these ideas critically, asking yourself how they align with your own values and what kind of future they may create. Whether you see Project 2025 as the path to restoring America's greatness or as a potential threat to longstanding democratic institutions, it's clear that this initiative is not one to be ignored.

Chapter 1: Reshaping Government Structure

Imagine a government where the President has more direct control over every facet of federal operations, where civil servants are handpicked based on political alignment, and where the vast bureaucracies of Washington are radically restructured—or even dismantled entirely. This is the future that *Project 2025* envisions, a vision that fundamentally reshapes the structure of the federal government, starting with sweeping reforms in the federal workforce and culminating in the expansion of executive power.

As you read through this chapter, you'll explore the key components of *Project 2025's* blueprint for governance. By the end, you'll understand why this proposal could either be seen as a necessary step to reclaim efficient government or a dangerous overreach that threatens the balance of power in America.

Federal Workforce Reforms

One of the boldest aspects of *Project 2025* is its proposal to fire thousands of federal employees and replace them with individuals aligned with conservative values. This isn't just about trimming fat from the government; it's about fundamentally altering who runs the country's administrative machinery. Proponents argue that too many federal agencies are staffed by bureaucrats with liberal or progressive leanings, making it difficult for any conservative administration to implement its policies. By placing conservative-aligned personnel in key positions, the aim is to ensure that the federal workforce is not just neutral but actively supportive of a conservative agenda.

But what does this mean to you, the everyday American? At first glance, this plan may seem like a way to make the government more responsive to the will of the people. After all, if the President is elected by the majority, shouldn't the people working under him or her be aligned with the policies that were voted for?

Yet, beneath the surface, this approach raises fundamental concerns about the neutrality of the civil service. Historically, civil servants are meant to be nonpartisan professionals who carry out the will of any administration, regardless of political leaning. They are the backbone of governance, ensuring continuity even as presidents and congressmen come and go. By filling these positions with ideologically aligned personnel, *Project 2025* risks turning what was once a neutral administrative apparatus into an extension of a specific political ideology.

You might be wondering: Is that such a bad thing? If you believe in conservative principles, perhaps you see this as a long-overdue correction to a left-leaning bureaucracy. But imagine the implications if the tables were turned. If a future liberal administration adopted the same approach, staffing the federal workforce entirely with progressives, you might begin to question the impartiality of government services.

It's essential to recognize that firing thousands of federal employees isn't just a logistical challenge—it's a move that could create instability within the government. Civil servants have expertise and institutional knowledge that helps keep the government functioning smoothly. Replacing them en masse could lead to a chaotic transition period where key tasks are delayed, programs are mismanaged, and the quality of public services deteriorates. For you, this could mean longer wait times for essential services, a reduction in the effectiveness of programs you rely on, or a lack of continuity in critical areas like public health or disaster response.

Moreover, the idea of replacing career civil servants with politically aligned personnel undermines the very concept of a merit-based bureaucracy. Traditionally, federal employees are selected based on qualifications and experience, not political affiliation. In contrast, *Project 2025* prioritizes ideology over competence, potentially putting individuals in positions of power not because they are the most qualifed but because they support the administration's worldview.

While it's true that every administration seeks to bring in its own leadership, typically in high-level positions, *Project 2025* goes much further, aiming to re-engineer the entire civil service to be politically aligned. This shift has long-term implications for governance because it makes it more difficult for future administrations, especially those with differing views, to operate effectively.

The neutrality of the civil service is not just a bureaucratic concern; it's a pillar of American democracy. It ensures that government functions are carried out fairly, regardless of which political party is in power. You might not think much about civil service neutrality in your day-to-day life, but consider this: if federal agencies start to become heavily politicized, can you be sure that decisions are being made in the public interest, rather than in the interest of a particular political agenda?

For example, agencies like the Environmental Protection Agency (EPA) or the Department of Justice (DOJ) are tasked with making decisions that impact millions of Americans. If these agencies become populated with individuals selected for their ideological views rather than their expertise, the policies they enforce could become less about what's best for the country and more about what's best for a particular political party. This risks creating a government that serves only those who are politically aligned with the administration, rather than all citizens equally.

Furthermore, the ripple effect of a politicized civil service could extend into every corner of governance. Imagine how this could affect the way federal grants are distributed, how environmental regulations are enforced, or how public health guidelines are crafted. Decisions by federal agencies often have a direct impact on your community, your job, and even your health. When these decisions are driven by ideology rather than evidence and expertise, the consequences can be far-reaching and deeply personal.

Expanding Executive Power

One of the core components of *Project 2025* is the dramatic expansion of executive power. In essence, the project proposes a government where the president holds significantly more authority over federal agencies, reducing bureaucratic red tape and allowing for swift, decisive action. This concentration of power would come at the expense of Congress, the judiciary, and the civil service—institutions traditionally tasked with providing checks and balances on the executive branch.

The argument for expanding executive power is simple. In an era of polarized politics and gridlock, the president needs more direct control to implement policies efficiently. You've probably seen how slow Congress can be to pass legislation, and the idea of cutting through bureaucracy to get things done may appeal to you. After all, who wouldn't want a more responsive, effective government?

Yet, this concentration of power in the executive branch comes with risks. The American political system was designed with a delicate balance of powers. The Founding Fathers intentionally distributed authority across three branches of government—executive, legislative and judicial—to prevent any one branch from becoming too powerful. By concentrating power within the presidency, *Project 2025* risks upsetting this balance, making it more difficult for Congress or the courts to serve as a check on executive overreach.

You may think that expanding executive power is a good thing when the president shares your values, but what happens when the office is held by someone whose views you don't agree with? Power, once expanded, rarely contracts. A president from the opposite political party could use these enhanced powers in ways that conflict with your beliefs. In a government where the president holds unchecked authority, your voice—and the voices of millions of other Americans—could become marginalized.

Moreover, increasing executive power diminishes the role of Congress, the institution most directly accountable to the people. Congress is composed of elected representatives who are supposed to reflect the will of their constituents. By sidelining Congress, *Project 2025* weakens the link between the government and the electorate, making it harder for ordinary citizens like you to influence the direction of the country through your vote.

Concentrating Power to Reduce Bureaucracy

One of the primary reasons *Project 2025* advocates for the expansion of executive power is to reduce bureaucracy. Government agencies are often criticized for being slow, inefficient, and resistant to change. You've likely experienced the frustrations of dealing with government red tape, whether you're applying for a permit, trying to access benefits, or navigating the complexities of the tax system. The promise of cutting through that red tape is understandably appealing.

By giving the president more control over federal agencies, *Project 2025* aims to streamline decision-making and eliminate bureaucratic obstacles. In theory, this could lead to a more efficient government that's better able to respond to the needs of the people. However, efficiency shouldn't come at the cost of accountability.

Bureaucracy, for all its flaws, serves an important function: it provides a buffer between political leaders and the implementation of policy. This buffer ensures that policies are carried out in a fair, impartial manner, based on the rule of law rather than the whims of political leaders. When you eliminate or weaken this buffer, you open the door to abuses of power.

For example, imagine a scenario in which the president can unilaterally direct the IRS to audit political opponents or instruct federal law enforcement to selectively enforce laws. These scenarios may sound extreme, but without sufficient checks on executive power, they become possibilities. A government without bureaucratic checks may be more efficient, but it's also more susceptible to corruption and abuse.

Impact on Government Accountability and Democratic Checks and Balances

Expanding executive power and reducing bureaucracy have a direct impact on government accountability. In a system where the president holds unchecked power, it becomes harder for citizens to hold their government accountable. You might think that this doesn't affect you directly, but consider how difficult it would be to challenge government decisions or policies that you disagree with when those decisions are made without input from Congress or oversight from the courts.

Accountability is central to democratic governance. You elect representatives to Congress to represent your interests and ensure that the executive branch doesn't overstep its bounds. But in a system where executive power is concentrated, those representatives lose their ability to serve as an effective check on the president. This weakens your ability to influence the country's direction through democratic means.

Moreover, *Project 2025's* focus on reducing Congress' role in governance challenges the fundamental principles of checks and balances that have defined the American political system for over two centuries. The Founding Fathers understood that power tends to undoubtedly corrupt. That's why they created a system of checks and balances, where the power of each branch of government—executive, legislative, and judicial—serves to limit the power of the others. By concentrating more power in the executive branch, *Project 2025* erodes this delicate balance, making it easier for the president to bypass Congress and the courts in pursuing his or her agenda.

Consider the implications of this for democratic accountability. When power is concentrated in the hands of one individual, it becomes more difficult for you, as a citizen, to influence government decisions. Congress, which represents you and your neighbors, would have less say in how the country is run. Judges, who interpret the Constitution and ensure that laws are applied fairly, would have less authority to check executive actions. This shift toward executive dominance weakens the mechanisms that have traditionally safeguarded American democracy.

Consequences for Democratic Participation

The concentration of executive power proposed by *Project 2025* could also have a chilling effect on democratic participation. You may feel that your voice matters less if the president can unilaterally make decisions without the input of Congress or consultation with the public. This could lead to voter apathy and disengagement, as people may feel that their representatives in Congress no longer have the power to advocate on their behalf.

Moreover, the increased power of the executive branch could limit the effectiveness of protests, petitions, and other forms of democratic engagement. In a system where the president holds significant control over federal agencies, there may be fewer avenues for you to challenge government actions or influence policy decisions. This centralization of power makes it more difficult for grassroots movements to hold the government accountable and ensures that fewer checks exist to curb potential abuses of power.

Project 2025 promises to reshape the federal government in a way that concentrates power in the hands of the president, reduces the role of Congress, and replaces civil servants with ideologically aligned personnel. For supporters of conservative policies, this may seem like a necessary correction to decades of perceived government overreach. But for many, it represents a dangerous erosion of democratic checks and balances, a shift that could weaken accountability, politicize the civil service, and diminish the role of the American people in their own government.

You might see the appeal of streamlining government and reducing bureaucracy, but you must also consider the long-term consequences of concentrating power in the executive branch. When power is concentrated, it is harder to reverse, and you may find yourself living in a system where democratic accountability is significantly weakened. Even if you agree with the policies proposed by *Project 2025*, it's important to ask yourself whether these reforms are worth the price of reducing the checks and balances that have kept American democracy resilient for more than two centuries.

In a government reshaped by *Project 2025*, you may find that the levers of power are no longer as accessible as they once were. The decisions that impact your life—whether they involve healthcare, taxes, or environmental protections—will be made by a government that is less accountable to you and more aligned with a single political ideology. As you reflect on the vision laid out in *Project 2025*, consider not just the short-term gains but the long-term implications for the balance of power in the American government. After all, democracy is not just about who holds power today, but about ensuring that the system remains fair and accountable for generations to come.

Chapter 2: Taxation and Economic Policy

Imagine waking up to a tax system that fundamentally reshapes the way wealth is distributed in the country, a system that promises simplicity and fairness, but one that also deepens the divide between the rich and everyone else. This is what *Project 2025* envisions with its proposed tax overhaul. It aims to revamp the tax code by introducing a two-rate tax system and slashing corporate tax rates, all in the name of fostering economic growth and increasing efficiency. But as you dig deeper into these changes, you might start to wonder: who truly benefits from this new tax structure, and what does it mean for you, your family, and your community?

In this chapter, we will examine the proposed tax reforms outlined in *Project 2025*, focusing on the introduction of a two-rate tax system and the reduction of corporate taxes. We'll explore how these changes could benefit high earners and large corporations, and what the implications are for middle- and lower-income Americans. By the end, you will have a clear understanding of how these policies could reshape the economy and widen the gap between the haves and the have-nots.

Tax Overhaul: A Two-Rate System

Central to *Project 2025*'s tax reform is the introduction of a two-rate individual income tax system. Under this plan, the current progressive tax system—with its seven brackets ranging from 10% to 37%—would be replaced with just two rates: 15% and 30%. This move is designed to simplify the tax code and reduce what supporters see as excessive taxation on high earners and businesses. But is this really true, and what does it mean for you?

You might be thinking, *simpler taxes sound great!*. After all, who wouldn't want to replace the confusing web of tax brackets and deductions with a system that's easier to understand? However, as with most things in government policy, the devil is in the details. While a simpler tax system may seem appealing, it's crucial to consider how it affects different income groups.

The first thing to note is that under the current system, the tax rate increases as your income goes up. This means higher earners pay a larger percentage of their income in taxes, which is a key feature of a progressive tax system. In contrast, *Project 2025's* proposed two-rate system would flatten the tax burden, offering a much lower top rate (30%) than the current highest rate (37%). For those in the highest income bracket, this represents a significant tax cut. If you're a high earner, this might sound like welcome news, but for most Americans—especially those in the middle- and lower-income brackets—the story is quite different.

So who benefits most from this tax overhaul? The answer is clear: high-income individuals and wealthy households. By reducing the top rate to 30%, *Project 2025* essentially gives the richest Americans a significant tax break. Meanwhile, those in the middle-income range might not see much of a change, and some could even end up paying more, especially if the elimination of certain deductions and credits disproportionately affects them.

One of the most notable aspects of *Project 2025's* tax plan is its intention to eliminate various deductions and credits that currently benefit middle- and lower-income households. For example, deductions for mortgage interest, state and local taxes, and education expenses could be on the chopping block. While these deductions might seem insignificant in the grand scheme of things, they provide crucial relief for many families. If you're a homeowner, for instance, the mortgage interest deduction could mean the difference between a manageable tax bill and one that eats into your savings. Without these deductions, you could end up paying more in taxes, even if your income falls within the lower 15% tax bracket.

The Effects on Different Income Groups

It's important to understand how this tax overhaul affects different income groups. If you're a high-income earner, *Project 2025* offers you a clear benefit: lower taxes and fewer restrictions on how you manage your wealth. The elimination of deductions might not affect you as much because you have more disposable income to absorb the impact.

But what if you're not a high earner? How does this plan affect middle- and lower-income families? **You might find yourself asking**, *How is this fair?* Middle-income earners may see fewer benefits from the two-rate system, and those in lower income brackets might actually see their tax burden increase, depending on which deductions and credits are eliminated. In essence, while the two-rate system might reduce the complexity of the tax code, it also risks shifting more of the tax burden onto those who are already struggling to make ends meet.

For lower-income households, the elimination of key tax credits—such as the Earned Income Tax Credit (EITC)—could be particularly devastating. The EITC has long been a lifeline for working families, providing much-needed tax relief to those who earn less but still work hard to support their families. By reducing or eliminating this credit, *Project 2025* would make it harder for millions of low-income Americans to climb the economic ladder.

You might wonder, *Is there any justification for this shift in the tax burden?* Proponents of *Project 2025* argue that cutting taxes for high earners and corporations will stimulate economic growth, create jobs, and boost wages. But the evidence is mixed. While it's true that lower taxes can lead to more investment and economic activity, the benefits of such growth often don't trickle down to those who need them most. Instead, the rich get richer, while everyone else struggles to keep up.

Corporate Tax Reduction

Besides overhauling individual income taxes, *Project 2025* proposes a significant reduction in corporate taxes. Under the plan, the corporate tax rate would be slashed from 21% to 18%. For corporations and their shareholders, this is a major victory. But for the average American worker, the consequences are far less clear.

You might ask, *How does lowering corporate taxes affect me?* The argument in favor of corporate tax cuts is that they will lead to increased investment, higher wages, and more jobs. After all, if businesses have more money to invest, they're more likely to expand, hire new workers, and raise salaries. But the reality is more complicated.

In recent years, we've seen that corporate tax cuts don't always lead to the promised benefits for workers. Instead of using their tax savings to hire more employees or raise wages, many corporations choose to invest in stock buybacks, which boost the value of their shares and disproportionately benefit wealthy shareholders. If you're part of the top 1% of earners, this is great news. But if you're a middle-class worker, you may not see much of an impact on your paycheck.

In fact, there's a growing body of evidence that corporate tax cuts exacerbate income inequality rather than reduce it. **You might be wondering**, *How does this happen?* When corporations use their tax savings to enrich shareholders rather than invest in their workforce, the gap between the rich and everyone else widens. Wealthy investors and corporate executives reap the benefits of stock buybacks and rising share prices, while workers see little to no improvement in their wages or job security.

And then there's the issue of government revenue. By reducing the corporate tax rate from 21% to 18%, *Project 2025* would significantly reduce the amount of money flowing into the federal government. This shortfall would need to be made up elsewhere, either through higher taxes on individuals or cuts to essential government programs like Social Security, Medicare, and public education. **You might ask yourself**, *Is this trade-off worth it?* Lowering corporate taxes may boost profits for large companies, but if it comes at the expense of vital public services, the benefits may be short-lived and unequally distributed.

The Impact on Economic Inequality

One of the most significant consequences of *Project 2025*'s tax and economic policy is its potential to deepen economic inequality. While high earners and corporations stand to gain the most from these reforms, middle- and lower-income Americans could be left behind.

You might be thinking, *How does this affect me?* If you're in the middle class, the reduction in corporate taxes and the flattening of the individual tax brackets might not offer much immediate relief. In fact, you could see a decline in the quality of public services as the government struggles to balance its budget in the wake of reduced revenue.

For those in the lower-income brackets, the outlook is ever more concerning. Without access to tax credits and deductions that have traditionally provided a buffer against economic hardship, millions of Americans could find themselves paying a larger share of their income in taxes, even as the wealthy enjoy substantial tax breaks.

The corporate tax cuts proposed by *Project 2025* also contribute to this growing inequality. When corporations use their tax savings to increase stock buybacks and boost executive pay, the gap between the rich and the rest of society widens. The wealthy, who hold the majority of stock market investments, see their wealth grow exponentially, while the average worker struggles to keep up.

Corporate Behavior and Economic Policy

Reducing corporate taxes isn't just about tax savings; it's also about shaping corporate behavior. Proponents of *Project 2025* argue that lowering the corporate tax rate will encourage businesses to invest in the U.S., create jobs, and increase wages. But the track record of corporate tax cuts suggests otherwise.

You might ask, *Why aren't corporations reinvesting their tax savings in their workers?* The answer lies in the nature of corporate incentives. In today's economy, corporations are more focused on short-term profits and shareholder value than on long-term investments in their workforce. Stock buybacks, which**Corporate Behavior and Economic Policy**

Reducing corporate taxes is not just about tax savings; it's also about shaping corporate behavior. Proponents of *Project 2025* argue that lowering the corporate tax rate will encourage businesses to reinvest their savings into the economy, create more jobs, and increase wages for workers. It sounds like a win-win situation: corporations thrive, and the benefits trickle down to everyday Americans. But if you dig deeper, you'll see that the reality is far more complex.

In recent years, after previous corporate tax cuts, many businesses choose not to reinvest their tax savings into expanding their workforce or raising wages. Instead, they focused on short-term gains like stock buybacks. Stock buybacks artificially inflate the value of a company's shares, making investors and executives wealthier while doing little to boost wages or job growth. **You might be wondering**, *Why aren't corporations using their tax savings to invest in workers?* The answer lies in corporate incentives. In today's economy, corporations are often more focused on maximizing shareholder value than investing in long-term growth or workforce development.

What does this mean for you? If you're a middle-class worker, you might not see the benefits of these corporate tax cuts reflected in your paycheck. While corporations and their wealthy shareholders become richer, wage growth remains stagnant for many Americans. This exacerbates economic inequality, as those at the top continue to accumulate wealth while everyone else struggles to keep up.

Additionally, corporate tax cuts reduce the amount of revenue that the government collects. **You might think**, *Why should I care if the government collects less money?* But think about the services that government revenue funds: education, infrastructure, healthcare, and social safety nets like Social Security and Medicare. When the government collects less revenue from corporations, it has to make up for that shortfall elsewhere—often by cutting public services or raising taxes on individuals.

The Potential Impact on Government Revenue

You might ask, *How does lowering corporate taxes affect the federal budget?* It's simple: when corporations pay less in taxes, the government collects less revenue. According to *Project 2025*, the corporate tax rate would be reduced from 21% to 18%, which might seem like a small decrease but could lead to significant revenue losses for the federal government. This is revenue that could have been used to fund public schools, healthcare programs, infrastructure projects, or even pay down the national debt.

But how does the government make up for this lost revenue? One option is to raise taxes on individuals, particularly middle- and lower-income Americans. Another option is to cut spending on essential programs like education, healthcare, and social safety nets. Either way, the burden is shifted onto regular people—people like you—who might already be struggling to make ends meet.

You might be asking, *Isn't it worth the trade-off if corporate tax cuts create more jobs?* Unfortunately, evidence does not always support this claim. While some businesses might reinvest their tax savings into expanding operations and hiring more workers, many others will prioritize stock buybacks or executive bonuses. This means that the benefits of corporate tax cuts often go to wealthy investors and corporate executives, rather than to workers or the broader economy.

Economic Inequality and the Wealth Gap

The combination of individual tax cuts for the wealthy and corporate tax cuts will almost certainly increase economic inequality in the United States. **You might wonder**, *How does this happen?* When the rich receive large tax breaks, they tend to save or invest the extra money, rather than spend it. This leads to an accumulation of wealth among the top 1%, while middle- and lower-income Americans struggle to keep up with rising costs of living and stagnant wages.

Meanwhile, corporate tax cuts disproportionately benefit large corporations and their shareholders, many of whom are already wealthy. When these corporations use their tax savings to buy back stock or pay dividends to shareholders, the wealth gap widens even further. **You might be thinking**, *But don't these policies stimulate the economy?* While tax cuts can lead to short-term economic growth, the long-term effects are often increased inequality and a greater concentration of wealth at the top.

For most Americans, the reality is that these tax cuts do little to improve their financial situation. The benefits of corporate tax cuts and a simplified tax system largely flow to the wealthiest individuals and corporations, leaving middle- and lower-income families to bear the brunt of any lost government revenue through higher taxes or reduced services.

You might ask, *What are the long-term consequences of this tax overhaul?* While corporate tax cuts and a flatter individual tax system may stimulate short-term economic growth, the long-term consequences could be damaging to economic stability. As wealth becomes more concentrated among the rich, consumer demand from middle- and lower-income families—who spend a larger percentage of their income—could stagnate or even decline. This lack of consumer demand could, in turn, slow economic growth and lead to a cycle of economic stagnation.

Furthermore, reducing government revenue by cutting corporate taxes makes it harder for the government to invest in critical infrastructure projects, education, and healthcare. **You might wonder**, *Why should I care about government spending?* The answer is simple: public investments in things like education and infrastructure benefit everyone by creating jobs, improving public health, and making it easier for businesses to operate. When the government cuts spending in these areas to make up for lost revenue from corporate tax cuts, it harms the economy in the long run.

Conclusion: A Tax System for the Wealthy?

Project 2025's tax proposals might sound appealing at first glance: a simpler tax system, lower rates for individuals and corporations, and the promise of economic growth. But when you look closer, it's clear that these reforms primarily benefit high earners and large corporations, while doing little to help middle- and lower-income Americans. In fact, the proposed tax changes could increase economic inequality, weaken public services, and make it harder for ordinary people to get ahead.

As you consider the implications of these tax reforms, it's important to ask yourself: **Who benefits most from these policies?** If you're in the top 1%, *Project 2025* offers you substantial tax breaks and fewer government regulations. But if you're like most Americans, you might find yourself paying more in taxes, receiving fewer services, and struggling to make ends meet in an economy that increasingly favors the wealthy.

In the end, the question isn't just about taxes—it's about what kind of society we want to live in. **Do we want a society where wealth is concentrated at the top, while public services are starved of funding? Or do we want a society where everyone has the opportunity to succeed, and where the government plays a role in ensuring fairness and equality?** The choices we make about taxation and economic policy will shape our country's future for generations to come.

Chapter 3: Immigration and Border Policies

When you think about the future of immigration in the United States, you might envision a system that's either more open or more restrictive, depending on your perspective. Immigration is one of the most contentious issues in modern politics, and *Project 2025* proposes a radical shift, envisioning a return to many of the policies established during the Trump administration. These policies, designed to tighten border security and limit the number of people who can enter the country, represent a significant departure from previous U.S. immigration policies, which emphasized humanitarian aid and family reunification. If implemented, these changes could fundamentally alter the landscape of immigration in America—and not necessarily for the better.

In this chapter, you will explore the proposed return of Trump-era immigration policies, including the tightening of asylum requirements, the reduction of refugee admissions, and the reinstatement of the Migrant Protection Protocols (also known as the Remain in Mexico policy). We will also examine how a shift to a merit-based immigration system could affect the diversity of the U.S. population and the composition of the workforce. Ultimately, *Project 2025* promises to reshape immigration policy, but at what cost? Let's dig deeper into what these changes would mean for immigrants, border communities, and industries that rely on immigrant labor.

Return of Trump-Era Immigration Policies

One of the key components of *Project 2025* is a return to many of the hardline immigration policies implemented during Donald Trump's presidency. These policies are designed to reduce the number of immigrants and refugees entering the United States and to more strictly enforce border security. If you support a more restrictive immigration policy, this might seem like a step in the right direction. But before you decide, it's worth considering the full impact of these policies, not just on immigrants but on the broader U.S. economy and society.

Under *Project 2025*, asylum requirements would be significantly tightened, making it more difficult for individuals fleeing persecution or violence to seek refuge in the U.S. The reasoning behind this is simple Proponents of these policies argue that the current asylum system is abused by individuals who are not truly fleeing persecution but are instead seeking economic opportunities. While it's true that the asylum system can be exploited, tightening the requirements so drastically could also mean turning away people who are in genuine need of protection.

You might ask yourself, *What's wrong with making asylum harder to obtain if it prevents fraud?* The problem is that by narrowing the criteria for asylum, the U.S. risks denying safe haven to individuals fleeing extreme violence, political persecution, or other life-threatening situations. If you were in their shoes, wouldn't you want the opportunity to seek refuge in a country that claims to uphold human rights and offer protection to those in need?

Beyond the moral implications, there's also a practical side to consider. Asylum seekers often contribute to the U.S. economy, taking on jobs in industries that are struggling to find workers. By limiting the number of people who can qualify for asylum, *Project 2025* could exacerbate labor shortages in sectors such as agriculture, construction, and hospitality—industries that have historically relied on imm grant labor to function smoothly.

Project 2025 also calls for reducing the number of refugees admitted to the United States. This policy would significantly cut back on the nation's role as a global leader in providing refuge to those fleeing war, famine, and persecution. You may be thinking, *Why should the U.S. bear the burden of resettling refugees when other countries can step up?* It's a valid question, but consider this: historically, the U.S. has taken in a larger share of refugees because of its vast resources, economic power, and commitment to global humanitarian efforts. Reducing the number of refugee admissions isn't just about saving money or reducing the strain on domestic resources. It also signals a retreat from the U.S.'s role on the world stage as a champion of human rights.

For decades, the U.S. has been a place where refugees could rebuild their lives and contribute to the American economy. Refugees often work hard to integrate into their new communities, and many go on to start businesses, buy homes, and create jobs for other Americans. By slashing refugee admissions, *Project 2025* could deprive the U.S. of the economic and cultural contributions that refugees bring to the country.

Reinstating the Migrant Protection Protocols (Remain in Mexico Policy)

One of the most controversial Trump-era immigration policies was the Migrant Protection Protocols, commonly known as the Remain in Mexico policy. Under this policy, asylum seekers who arrived at the U.S. southern border were required to wait in Mexico while their cases were processed in U.S. immigration courts. Proponents of the policy argued that it reduced the number of immigrants entering the U.S. illegally and helped alleviate overcrowding at detention centers.

However, **you might wonder**, *What are the human costs of such a policy?* Critics of the Remain in Mexico policy point to the dangerous and unsanitary conditions many asylum seekers faced while waiting in Mexico. Migrants were often forced to live in makeshift camps with limited access to food, clean water, and medical care. Reports of violence, kidnapping, and exploitation in these camps were widespread, and many migrants found themselves stuck in limbo for months or even years as their asylum cases dragged on.

From a humanitarian perspective, the reinstatement of this policy would likely cause a return to these dire conditions. But there's also a broader economic impact to consider. By keeping asylum seekers in Mexico, the U.S. effectively shuts off a source of labor for industries that rely on immigrants to fill low-wage jobs. This is particularly true in border states like Texas, Arizona, and California, where industries such as agriculture and hospitality are heavily dependent on immigrant labor.

You may be wondering, *How do these stricter immigration policies affect the people living in border communities?* The truth is, border towns and cities have long been shaped by the flow of immigrants across the U.S.-Mexico border. Many of these communities have developed vibrant, binational economies where goods, services, and labor move fluidly across the border.

Tighter immigration controls could disrupt these economies, making it more difficult for businesses to find workers and for cross-border trade to continue. In cities like El Paso, Texas, and San Diego, California, businesses depend on a steady stream of customers and employees from Mexico. If immigration is restricted, these communities could suffer economically.

On a broader scale, the U.S. economy relies on immigrant labor in a variety of industries, from agriculture to healthcare. By restricting the number of immigrants allowed to enter the country, *Project 2025* could create labor shortages that drive up wages in some sectors. While higher wages might sound like a good thing, they could also lead to higher prices for goods and services, affecting everyone.

Merit-Based Immigration

Another key aspect of *Project 2025* is the transition from family-based immigration to a merit-based system. In a merit-based immigration system, individuals are selected to immigrate based on their skills, education, and ability to contribute to the economy. If you support the idea of attracting the "best and brightest" from around the world, this policy might seem like a good idea. After all, who wouldn't want to bring in immigrants who are highly skilled and can immediately contribute to the U.S. economy?

However, **you might ask**, *What are the downsides of this approach?* One of the main criticisms of merit-based immigration is that it prioritizes certain types of immigrants while devaluing the contributions of others. Under the current family-based system, many immigrants come to the U.S. to reunite with family members who are already citizens or

permanent residents. These immigrants may not all be highly educated
or highly skilled, but they still make valuable contributions to their
communities and the economy.

The Impact on Diversity

A merit-based immigration system would likely cause a less diverse
population. **You might wonder**, *How could this happen?* By focusing on
skills and education, the U.S. would likely attract immigrants from
wealthier countries that have better access to education and job training.
Immigrants from poorer countries—many of whom are fleeing violence,
poverty, or persecution—would have a harder time qualifying under a
merit-based system.

In the long run, this could cause a less diverse workforce and a less
diverse population. Immigrants from different backgrounds bring new
perspectives, ideas, and cultures that enrich American society. By
limiting immigration to those with certain skills, *Project 2025* could
reduce the diversity that has long been one of the country's greatest
strengths.

The Impact on Workforce Composition

From a workforce perspective, shifting to a merit-based immigration
system could have both positive and negative effects. On the positive
side, it could help fill gaps in high-skill industries like technology,
engineering, and healthcare, where there is often a shortage of qualified
workers. If you work in one of these industries, you might welcome the
influx of highly skilled immigrants who can help drive innovation and
economic growth.

But on the other hand, a merit-based system could create labor
shortages in industries that rely on lower-skilled workers. Sectors like
agriculture, construction, and food service are heavily dependent on
immigrant labor, much of which comes from family-based immigration. If
fewer immigrants are allowed into the country because they don't meet
the criteria of a merit-based system, these industries could struggle to
find enough workers to meet demand.

You might be thinking, *Why should I care if there are fewer workers in low-wage industries?* The answer is simple: labor shortages in these industries can lead to higher prices for the goods and services you rely on. If farmers can't find enough workers to harvest their crops, for example, thelf farmers can't find enough workers to harvest their crops, for example, the prices of fruits and vegetables could rise, and you'd feel the impact at the grocery store. Similarly, construction delays due to labor shortages could lead to higher housing costs, making it more expensive for you and your family to buy or rent a home. In industries like food service and hospitality, labor shortages could cause longer wait times, reduced service quality, and higher prices.

You might ask, *Is there a way to balance merit-based immigration with the need for low-skilled workers?* One possible solution is to create a hybrid immigration system that allows both types of immigrants. While merit-based immigration can help fill gaps in high-skilled industries, family-based immigration and refugee programs ensure that there is a steady supply of workers in industries that rely on lower-skilled labor. By maintaining a balance between the two systems, the U.S. could meet the needs of its economy while still upholding its humanitarian commitments.

The Broader Impacts on American Society

Beyond the immediate effects on immigrants, border communities, and industries reliant on immigrant labor, *Project 2025*'s immigration policies have broader implications for American society. By tightening asylum requirements, reducing refugee admissions, and shifting to a merit-based immigration system, these policies signal a retreat from the values of openness and inclusivity that have long defined the United States.

You might wonder, *What kind of message does this send to the world?* By closing the door to refugees and asylum seekers, the U.S. risks losing its reputation as a beacon of hope for those fleeing persecution and violence. This could have far-reaching consequences for the country's standing on the world stage, as other nations might question America's commitment to human rights and global leadership.

At the same time, the focus on merit-based immigration could deepen existing divides within American society. While highly skilled immigrants are certainly valuable contributors to the economy, prioritizing them over other types of immigrants sends the message that only certain types of people are welcome in the U.S. This could exacerbate social tensions and fuel divisions along class, race and nationality lines.

You might be asking, *Is there a way to reform immigration policy without sacrificing the values of inclusivity and compassion?* One possible approach is to create a more flexible immigration system that addresses both economic and humanitarian concerns. This could involve maintaining robust asylum and refugee programs while also expanding opportunities for merit-based immigration. By striking a balance between these different priorities, the U.S. could build an immigration system that reflects both its economic needs and its core values.

Conclusion: The Future of Immigration in America

As you consider the immigration policies outlined in *Project 2025*, it's important to weigh the potential benefits against the costs. While tighter border controls and a merit-based immigration system might seem like sensible solutions to the challenges of immigration, they also come with significant trade-offs. Immigrants, border communities, industries reliant on immigrant labor, and the broader fabric of American society would all feel the impact of these policies in profound ways.

Ultimately, the question is not just about who gets to come to America—it's about what kind of country the U.S. wants to be. **Do we want to be a nation that welcomes diversity and provides opportunities for all, or do we want to retreat into isolation and exclusivity?** The choices we make about immigration policy will shape the future of the United States for generations to come, and it's up to you to decide which path is the right one.

Chapter 4: Social Safety Nets and Welfare

Imagine living in a society where the safety nets designed to help vulnerable populations—children, low-income families, and the elderly—are gradually dismantled. Where work requirements are added to essential welfare programs like Medicaid and SNAP, and where school meal programs and early childhood education opportunities, such as Head Start, are significantly reduced or eliminated. This is the vision *Project 2025* presents, a radical shift in how America handles welfare and social safety nets.

For you, as someone living in the United States, these changes could mean different things depending on your situation. If you're a middle- or high-income earner, you might not feel the immediate impact. But if you're part of a low-income family or someone who depends on these programs to make ends meet, *Project 2025*'s proposed welfare reforms could drastically alter your ability to access basic services like healthcare, food, and education. In this chapter, we'll explore the key components of these changes, focusing on the addition of work requirements for welfare programs, the reduction of access to school meal programs, and the push to reallocate funds toward at-home childcare rather than universal daycare programs.

Welfare Cuts and Work Requirements

One of the central proposals in *Project 2025* is adding work requirements to programs like Medicaid, SNAP (Supplemental Nutrition Assistance Program), and other forms of public assistance. The argument behind this policy is simple: proponents believe that requiring work for welfare benefits encourages personal responsibility, reduces dependency, and ultimately helps individuals escape poverty. But is it really that straightforward?

You might ask yourself, *How could work requirements improve the lives of those in need?* On the surface, requiring able-bodied individuals to work in exchange for government assistance seems like a reasonable expectation. After all, work is fundamental to self-sufficiency, and proponents argue that these policies would incentivize more people to join the workforce, reducing the overall strain on public welfare systems.

They envision a scenario where fewer people rely on government aid and more people are empowered to support themselves and their families.

However, the reality of work requirements is far more complex. **You may wonder**, *What happens to people who cannot find stable jobs or who have health issues that prevent them from working full-time?* For many low-income families, particularly those in rural or economically depressed areas, finding consistent employment is not as simple as it sounds. Many regions lack sufficient job opportunities, especially for those without higher education or specialized skills. Moreover, some individuals who rely on Medicaid or SNAP are already working, but their jobs are either part-time or pay wages too low to cover basic needs.

What happens when these families can't meet the work requirement? In many cases, they risk losing access to essential services. Imagine losing your healthcare coverage or your ability to buy groceries simply because you couldn't find a job that met the required number of hours. This isn't just about the inconvenience of losing benefits; for many, it's a matter of life and death. Without Medicaid, people with chronic illnesses like diabetes or heart disease might not be able to afford necessary medications. Without SNAP, children in low-income families could go hungry, exacerbating already precarious living conditions.

Moreover, work requirements tend to disproportionately affect individuals who are already vulnerable. **You might be thinking**, *If work requirements push people into jobs, doesn't that improve their lives?* But consider this: many people who rely on welfare are caregivers, either for young children or elderly family members. For these individuals, full-time employment outside the home may be impossible, and penalizing them by cutting off access to healthcare or food benefits only compounds their hardship.

In addition, the administrative burden of enforcing work requirements often falls on the very systems that are supposed to help people. States that have implemented work requirements for Medicaid, for example, have found that the process of verifying employment status is costly and bureaucratically challenging. In Arkansas, one of the first states to implement Medicaid work requirements, tens of thousands of people lost coverage—not because they refused to work, but because they couldn't navigate the confusing reporting system.

Alongside work requirements, *Project 2025* proposes cuts to critical programs that support children from low-income families. Specifically, the plan calls for reducing access to national school meal programs and the possible elimination of Head Start, an early childhood education program that serves nearly one million children across the U.S. each year.

You might ask, *Why cut these programs? Aren't they vital for children's development?* Proponents of these cuts argue that welfare programs like school meals and Head Start are inefficient and promote dependency. They believe that by cutting these programs, families will be forced to take greater responsibility for their children's needs and education. But what they fail to consider is the long-term impact that these cuts will have on children's health, academic achievement, and future opportunities.

Let's start with school meals. **You might not realize how** crucial free and reduced-price school lunches are for millions of American children. For many students, the meal they receive at school is the most nutritious—and sometimes the only—meal they get all day. Cutting access to school meal programs doesn't just mean that more children will go hungry; it also means that those children are less likely to concentrate in class, less likely to perform well academically, and more likely to face long-term health problems like obesity or malnutrition.

The impact on children's academic performance is well-documented. Studies have shown that children who are hungry or malnourished are more likely to struggle in school, leading to poorer grades, lower graduation rates, and fewer opportunities for upward mobility. **You might ask**, *Is it really fair to ask children to pay the price for budget cuts?* The answer, of course, is no. Children who rely on these programs have no control over their family's economic situation, and punishing them by cutting off access to nutritious meals is not only unfair but also shortsighted.

Now, let's talk about Head Start. This program has been a lifeline for low-income families since its inception in 1965. It provides early childhood education, health screenings, and parental support for families who would otherwise struggle to afford these services. **You might be wondering**, *Why eliminate Head Start?* Critics of the program argue that its outcomes are mixed and that many children who participate in Head Start do not maintain the academic gains they make in the program once they enter elementary school. But this argument ignores the broader benefits of Head Start, including the support it provides to families and the opportunities it creates for children to start school on a more level playing field.

For working parents, especially mothers, Head Start provides affordable childcare, enabling them to maintain jobs and contribute to their family's income. Without this support, many parents, particularly single mothers, would be forced to either reduce their hours or leave the workforce entirely, putting further strain on their already limited resources. Cutting Head Start, then, isn't just an attack on early childhood education—it's an attack on working families and gender equality.

Incentivizing At-Home Childcare

One of the most controversial aspects of *Project 2025* is its proposal to reallocate funds from universal daycare programs to incentivize at-home childcare. The reasoning behind this policy is that by encouraging parents—especially mothers—to stay home and care for their children, the government can reduce the need for costly daycare services while promoting family values and child development. On the surface, this might seem like a positive development for families who prefer to raise their children at home. But the broader implications are far more complicated.

You might ask, *Why wouldn't this be good for working parents?* After all, if you're a parent who wants to stay home with your children, receiving financial support from the government might sound appealing. However, by shifting funds away from universal daycare programs, *Project 2025* effectively limits the options available to working parents, especially mothers.

Consider this: in many families, both parents must work to make ends meet. If affordable, high-quality daycare is not available, one parent—most often the mother—may be forced to leave the workforce to care for the children. While this might be a viable option for some families, it has significant implications for women's economic independence and long-term career prospects.

You might be thinking, *Isn't it good for mothers to stay home with their children?* There's no doubt that parents should have the freedom to choose what works best for their families. But for many women, staying home is not a choice—it's an economic necessity. By reallocating funds away from universal daycare, *Project 2025* undermines the progress women have made in the workforce and reinforces traditional gender roles that limit women's ability to achieve economic independence and professional success.

In addition, incentivizing at-home childcare can have long-term effects on gender equality in the workplace. **You might wonder**, *How does this impact the broader economy?* When women leave the workforce to care for their children, they not only lose income in the short term but also miss out on opportunities for career advancement and salary growth. Over time, this contributes to the persistent gender wage gap, as women who take time off to care for children often find it difficult to re-enter the workforce at the same level they left.

By prioritizing at-home childcare over universal daycare, *Project 2025* sends a clear message: the role of women is in the home, not in the workplace. **You might ask**, *Is this really the direction we want our society to move in?* For families who rely on two incomes to make ends meet, the lack of affordable daycare options can make it difficult to achieve financial stability. And for women who want to pursue careers while raising children, the absence of high-quality daycare can create insurmountable barriers to success.

Long-Term-term impacts of this policy could extend beyond individual families. When fewer women participate in the workforce, the overall economy suffers. You might ask, *Why does it matter if fewer women work?* Research has shown that increased female labor force participation leads to higher economic growth. When women are able to work, they contribute to the economy, increase household income, and reduce poverty rates. By reducing access to affordable daycare, *Project 2025* risks sidelining a significant portion of the labor force, thereby slowing economic growth and perpetuating gender inequality.

In addition, the lack of affordable childcare disproportionately affects low-income families, who are least able to afford private daycare services. **You might be wondering**, *How do these families cope without access to affordable childcare?* In many cases, parents are forced to rely on informal or unregulated childcare arrangements, which can be lower quality and less reliable. This can have negative consequences for children's development and safety, and for parents' ability to maintain stable employment.

The Consequences for Vulnerable Populations

The proposed welfare cuts and work requirements outlined in *Project 2025* would disproportionately affect low-income families, children, and vulnerable populations. **You might be asking**, *What happens to those who can't meet these new requirements?* For many low-income individuals, particularly those with health issues, disabilities, or caregiving responsibilities, meeting strict work requirements is simply not feasible. Without access to essential services like Medicaid and SNAP, these individuals risk falling further into poverty.

For children in low-income families, the consequences are particularly severe. Without access to school meal programs and early childhood education, these children are more likely to experience hunger, poor academic performance, and developmental delays. **You might think**, *Isn't it the responsibility of parents to provide for their children?* While it's true that parents play a central role in their children's well-being, the reality is that many families face economic challenges beyond their control. By cutting access to these critical programs, *Project 2025* punishes children for circumstances they have no control over, making it harder for them to succeed in school and in life.

As you reflect on the welfare reforms proposed by *Project 2025*, it's important to consider the long-term implications for families, children, and society as a whole. **You might ask yourself,** *Is it really worth the cost to dismantle programs that provide critical support to the most vulnerable members of our society?* While proponents of these reforms argue that they will reduce dependency on government aid and promote personal responsibility, the reality is that these cuts will likely push more families into poverty and limit opportunities for future generations.

You might wonder, *Is there a better way to reform welfare?* One possible approach is to focus on strengthening the safety net rather than cutting it. By investing in programs that help families access healthcare, nutritious food, and quality education, we can create a society where all individuals have the opportunity to thrive. Rather than penalizing those who struggle to find work or afford childcare, we should be looking for ways to lift people out of poverty and support their efforts to achieve financial independence.

Ultimately, the choices we make about social safety nets and welfare reflect our values as a society. **Do we want to live in a country where everyone has access to basic necessities like healthcare, food, and education, or do we want to create a system that leaves behind the most vulnerable among us?** The decisions we make today will shape the future for generations to come.

Chapter 5: Energy Policy and the Environment

Imagine a future where the U.S. is completely energy independent, gas prices are lower than ever, and the economy is booming with new jobs in the oil, gas, and coal industries. That's the vision *Project 2025* proposes, a future built on expanding domestic fossil fuel production while simultaneously removing environmental regulations that stand in the way of economic growth. For many, this might sound appealing—lower energy costs, less reliance on foreign oil, and more jobs. But at what cost? As you'll see, the push for energy independence and economic growth is not without significant consequences for the environment and public health. These consequences will shape the future of our climate, our air and water quality, and the long-term sustainability of the planet.

In this chapter, we will delve into the specifics of *Project 2025's* energy policy, examining its goal to expand domestic oil and gas production and its strategy of rolling back environmental regulations. By exploring these key initiatives, you'll understand how these policies aim to boost short-term economic growth while potentially undermining long-term environmental protection and climate action. The question is: can we afford these trade-offs?

Unleashing American Energy Production

At the heart of *Project 2025* is a drive to significantly expand domestic oil and gas production. The rationale behind this push is straightforward: by increasing the supply of energy from within U.S. borders, prices will fall, the country will no longer be dependent on foreign energy sources, and millions of jobs will be created in the fossil fuel industry. **You might be thinking**, *Wouldn't it be great to pay less at the pump and see our economy thrive?* While there's no denying that cheaper energy would benefit many Americans, the environmental and climate costs of ramping up fossil fuel production cannot be ignored.

Expanding Drilling and Fracking

To achieve these goals, *Project 2025* proposes opening up federal lands and offshore areas for drilling. This includes previously protected regions like the Arctic National Wildlife Refuge and parts of the Gulf of Mexico, which are home to delicate ecosystems and endangered species. Additionally, the plan seeks to remove barriers to hydraulic fracturing, or fracking, which has revolutionized oil and gas production in the U.S.

You might ask yourself, *Why should I care if we drill in more places?* The reality is that while increased drilling could lower energy costs, it comes with serious environmental risks. Offshore drilling, for example, increases the likelihood of catastrophic oil spills that devastate marine life and coastal economies, as we saw with the Deepwater Horizon spill in 2010. Onshore, fracking is associated with groundwater contamination, methane emissions, and even increased earthquake activity in certain areas. The more we rely on these extraction methods, the greater the environmental and public health risks.

The Environmental Costs

You might be wondering, *How does all this oil and gas production affect me?* Beyond the immediate dangers of spills and contamination, burning fossil fuels releases greenhouse gasses that contribute to climate change. Carbon dioxide and methane, two of the strongest greenhouse gasses, trap heat in the Earth's atmosphere, leading to rising global temperatures. This may seem abstract, but the effects are already being felt: more frequent and severe hurricanes, floods, wildfires, and droughts—all of which disrupt lives, destroy property, and strain public resources.

By prioritizing fossil fuel production, *Project 2025* would lock the U.S. into a high-emissions trajectory, making it nearly impossible to meet international climate commitments such as those outlined in the Paris Agreement. **You might think**, *But isn't it worth it to achieve energy independence?* The challenge is that energy independence achieved through fossil fuels comes with long-term costs: an increasingly unstable climate, public health crises, and the destruction of natural ecosystems.

Short-Term Gains, Long-Term Costs

While expanding fossil fuel production might lower energy prices in the short term, the long-term environmental costs are enormous. **You might ask**, *Is it worth sacrificing our environment for cheaper energy today?*

The answer depends on how much value you place on the planet's future. Climate change, driven by the continued use of fossil fuels, will lead to more extreme weather events, rising sea levels, and disrupted ecosystems—all of which will cost far more to mitigate and repair than the short-term gains from cheaper energy.

Moreover, as renewable energy technologies like wind and solar become more cost-effective and widespread, the U.S. risks being left behind in the global energy transition. **You might wonder**, *Shouldn't we be investing in renewable energy instead?* The future of energy is clearly shifting towards renewables, which are cleaner, more sustainable, and increasingly competitive in price. By doubling down on fossil fuels, *Project 2025* risks missing out on the economic opportunities of the green energy revolution.

Rolling Back Environmental Regulations

Another critical component of *Project 2025*'s energy policy is the rollback of environmental regulations that proponents believe hinder economic growth. These regulations, which protect clean air, clean water, and endangered species, are often viewed as barriers to business and industry. **You might ask**, *Why would anyone want to remove these protections?* The answer lies in the belief that deregulation will stimulate economic growth by reducing compliance costs for businesses, particularly in energy-intensive industries like oil, gas, and manufacturing.

However, **you might wonder**, *What are the real costs of deregulation?* While removing regulations may boost profits for some industries, the long-term consequences for public health and the environment are severe.

The Clean Water Act and Clean Air Act

Two of the key environmental laws targeted by *Project 2025* are the Clean Water Act and the Clean Air Act. These landmark laws have been in place for decades and are responsible for reducing pollution and protecting public health. **You might ask**, *Why are these laws so important?* The Clean Water Act ensures that industries cannot dump harmful pollutants into rivers, lakes, and streams, which provide drinking water for millions of Americans. Without these protections, toxic chemicals, heavy metals, and industrial waste could contaminate water supplies, leading to serious health problems like cancer, reproductive issues, and neurological disorders.

Similarly, the Clean Air Act sets limits on emissions from factories, power plants, and vehicles, reducing the amount of harmful pollutants released into the atmosphere. **You might not realize**, but air pollution contributes to respiratory diseases like asthma, bronchitis, and lung cancer. Rolling back air quality standards would allow industries to emit more pollutants, worsening air quality and putting vulnerable populations—such as children, the elderly, and those with pre-existing health conditions—at greater risk.

Impact on Public Health

You might be wondering, *How does deregulation affect me and my family?* By removing restrictions on industrial emissions and pollution, more toxins will enter the air and water, leading to higher rates of illness and disease. Poor air quality, for example, is linked to increased hospitalizations and respiratory deaths. And water contamination can lead to long-term health effects, particularly for children who are more susceptible to toxins in drinking water.

You might think, *But businesses will still act responsibly, right?* Unfortunately, history shows that without strict regulations, many industries prioritize profits over environmental protection. Without oversight, pollution increases, and the public—rather than the polluters—bears the cost of the resulting health and environmental damage.

Economic vs. Environmental Trade-Offs

Proponents of deregulation argue that rolling back environmental protections will lead to economic growth, but the reality is more complex. **You might ask**, *How does deregulation boost the economy?* By reducing the cost of compliance, businesses can invest more in expansion, hire more workers, and increase production. In theory, this leads to higher profits and a stronger economy.

However, **you might wonder**, *Is economic growth worth the environmental and health costs?* While deregulation may provide short-term economic benefits for certain industries, the long-term costs of environmental degradation and public health crises far outweigh these gains. Pollution cleanup, healthcare costs associated with pollution-related illnesses, and the loss of natural resources all impose significant financial burdens on society.

Additionally, **you might be thinking**, *Aren't there ways to grow the economy without harming the environment?* The answer is yes. Investing in renewable energy, energy efficiency, and green technologies offers a path to sustainable economic growth that doesn't compromise environmental protection or public health. By focusing on innovation in these areas, the U.S. can create jobs, reduce its carbon footprint, and maintain a healthy environment for future generations.

Conclusion: Can We Afford the Cost of Deregulation and Fossil Fuel Expansion?

As you consider the energy policies outlined in *Project 2025*, it's important to weigh the short-term benefits against the long-term costs. **You might ask yourself**, *Is it really worth it to expand fossil fuel production and roll back environmental regulations?* While lower energy prices and economic growth may sound appealing, the environmental and public health consequences of these policies could be devastating.

You might wonder, *Is there a better way forward?* The answer lies in balancing energy production with environmentalism. By investing in renewable energy, maintaining strong environmental regulations, and prioritizing public health, the U.S. can achieve both economic growth and environmental sustainability.

The choices we make about energy and the environment today will shape the world we leave for future generations. **Do we want a future where short-term economic gains come at the expense of a livable planet, or a future where innovation and sustainability go hand in**

hand? The path we choose will determine the kind of world we live in—and the kind of world we leave behind.

Chapter 6: Education Policy

Imagine a future where the control over your child's education is no longer in the hands of the federal government but shifted entirely to state and local authorities. On the surface, this might sound like a step toward community empowerment, with the idea that local governments are more in tune with the unique needs of their residents. However, when you dig deeper into what *Project 2025* envisions, this shift could exacerbate existing inequities in education, especially for low-income and minority communities. Additionally, the project proposes significant restrictions on gender and identity education, including banning discussions of gender identity and prohibiting transgender students from competing in sports aligned with their gender identity.

In this chapter, we will explore the potential impact of *Project 2025's* education policies on public schools, particularly in vulnerable communities, and the far-reaching social and psychological effects that the proposed gender and identity policies could have on students. By the end, you'll understand how these policies could reshape education, potentially deepening divisions and limiting opportunities for marginalized groups.

Reducing Federal Control Over Education

One of the key components of *Project 2025* is reducing federal oversight and shifting responsibility for education to state and local governments. This policy is rooted in the belief that local communities are best equipped to make decisions about their schools, free from federal mandates. **You might be thinking**, *Isn't it better for communities to have more control over their education systems?* While the idea of local control seems appealing, the reality is that this shift could have serious consequences, particularly for schools that rely on federal funding to provide essential services.

The Role of Federal Funding in Public Education

To understand the impact of reducing federal control, it's important to examine the role that federal funding plays in public education. Programs like Title I provide additional funding to schools that serve high percentages of low-income students, ensuring that these schools have the resources they need to offer a quality education. **You might not realize** how crucial this funding is for schools in underserved communities. In some districts, federal dollars account for a significant portion of the budget, making up for shortfalls in state and local funding.

If *Project 2025* succeeds in shifting control and funding to state and local governments, many schools, especially those in low-income areas, could face severe budget cuts. **You might ask**, *Why can't states and local governments make up the difference?* The answer lies in the wide disparities in wealth between different communities. Wealthier areas can raise more money through property taxes, while poorer districts often struggle to provide even basic services. Without federal support, these schools could see larger class sizes, outdated materials, fewer extracurricular activities, and less access to advanced placement (AP) courses and special education resources.

Impact on Low-Income and Minority Communities

The consequences of reducing federal control will be felt most strongly in low-income and minority communities. Historically, the federal government has played a key role in promoting educational equity, ensuring that students from disadvantaged backgrounds have access to the same opportunities as their more affluent peers. Programs like Title I, the Individuals with Disabilities Education Act (IDEA), and the federal school lunch program provide critical support to students who need it the most.

You might ask, *What happens when federal oversight is removed?* In practice, decentralizing control will likely deepen existing inequalities. States and local governments will have more freedom to allocate resources as they see fit, but this could mean that wealthier districts continue to thrive while poorer districts fall further behind. **You might think**, *Shouldn't local control lead to better outcomes?* In theory, it could—but in reality, it often leads to greater disparities. States that prioritize tax cuts over public services may divert funding away from education, leaving under-resourced schools without the support they need.

You might wonder, *How can we ensure that all students get a fair shot?* The federal government's role in education has been to level the playing field, ensuring that all students—regardless of their ZIP code—have access to a quality education. Without federal oversight, it will be much harder to address the systemic inequities that have long plagued the U.S. education system.

Gender and Identity Policies in Schools

In addition to reducing federal control over education, *Project 2025* proposes strict restrictions on how schools address gender and identity issues. Specifically, the plan seeks to ban gender-related education in schools and prohibit transgender students from participating in sports aligned with their gender identity. **You might be thinking**, *Why are these policies being introduced?* Proponents of these measures argue that they are necessary to protect children from exposure to topics they believe are inappropriate for the classroom and to maintain fairness in school athletics. However, the impact of these policies on students—particularly LGBTQ+ students—could be deeply harmful.

Banning Gender-Related Education

The first element of this policy is a ban on gender-related education in schools. **You might wonder**, *Why should schools teach about gender identity?* For many students, particularly those who identify as LGBTQ+, learning about gender and sexual orientation in school can be a crucial part of understanding themselves and feeling validated in their experiences. Inclusive education helps create a safe space where all students can thrive, regardless of their identity.

By banning gender-related education, *Project 2025* effectively erases the experiences of LGBTQ+ students from the classroom, sending a message that their identities are not valid. **You might ask**, *Why does this matter?* The social and psychological consequences of exclusion are significant. LGBTQ+ students already face higher rates of bullying, discrimination, and mental health challenges than their peers. When schools fail to provide inclusive education, they contribute to a climate of stigma and silence that can have long-term effects on students' mental health and well-being.

You might think, *Isn't it better for parents to handle these discussions?* While parents certainly play a critical role in their children's development, schools also have a responsibility to provide students with accurate, age-appropriate information. Gender identity and sexual orientation are part of the diversity of human experience, and schools are in a unique position to teach empathy, respect, and understanding.

Prohibiting Transgender Students from Competing in Sports

The second element of *Project 2025's* gender and identity policy is the prohibition on transgender students competing in sports teams that align with their gender identity. **You might be thinking**, *Isn't this about fairness in sports?* Proponents of this policy argue that allowing transgender girls to compete on girls' sports teams gives them an unfair advantage due to biological differences. However, this argument oversimplifies the issue and ignores the lived experiences of transgender students.

For transgender youth, participating in school sports is not just about competition—it's about inclusion and belonging. **You might ask**, *What happens when transgender students are excluded from sports?* Denying transgender students the opportunity to compete on teams aligned with their gender identity can lead to feelings of rejection, isolation, and shame. It sends a message that their identities are invalid and that they do not belong.

Moreover, **you might wonder**, *How common is this issue?* The number of transgender athletes in school sports is relatively small, and there is no evidence to suggest that their participation undermines the integrity of athletic competitions. Many states and school districts have already implemented inclusive policies that allow transgender students to participate in sports, and these policies have been successful in promoting fairness and inclusion.

You might ask, *Shouldn't schools focus on creating inclusive environments for all students?* Excluding transgender students from participating in sports aligned with their gender identity only serves to marginalize them further, reinforcing harmful stereotypes and creating an environment where discrimination is normalized.

The policies proposed by *Project 2025* will have significant social and psychological effects on students, particularly those who are already vulnerable. **You might ask yourself**, *What are the long-term consequences of these policies?* The answer is clear: when schools fail to provide inclusive education or support for marginalized students, the harm can be lasting and profound.

Impact on LGBTQ+ Students

For LGBTQ+ students, the policies outlined in *Project 2025* could be especially damaging. **You might be wondering**, *Why is this such a big deal?* Research has consistently shown that LGBTQ+ youth are at a higher risk of mental health issues, including depression, anxiety, and suicide, largely due to the discrimination and rejection they face. When schools fail to provide support and inclusive education, they contribute to a cycle of harm that can follow students throughout their lives.

You might ask, *How can schools make a difference?* Schools that adopt inclusive policies—such as teaching about gender identity, providing safe spaces for LGBTQ+ students, and allowing transgender students to participate in sports—create environments where all students feel valued and accepted. This not only improves mental health outcomes for LGBTQ+ youth but also fosters a culture of respect and empathy among all students.

Impact on School Environments

Beyond the individual effects on students, the policies proposed by *Project 2025* will have a broader impact on school environments as a whole. **You might wonder**, *How does this affect the overall school climate?* When schools exclude certain students or limit discussions about important topics like gender and identity, they create a culture of silence and exclusion. This can lead to increased bullying, discrimination, and a lack of understanding among students, making it harder for schools to be the safe, supportive environments they should be.

You might be asking, *Is there a better way to address these issues?* Instead of banning discussions of gender or excluding transgender students from sports, schools should focus on creating inclusive, supportive environments where all students can learn, grow, and thrive.

Conclusion: The Future of Education Under *Project 2025*

As you consider the education policies proposed in *Project 2025*, itAs you consider the education policies proposed in *Project 2025*, it becomes clear that while the project seeks to give more power to local governments and address certain cultural issues in schools, these changes may have significant unintended consequences. Shifting control over education to state and local authorities could deepen existing disparities, particularly in low-income and minority communities, where federal funding has historically played a critical role in leveling the playing field. Additionally, the proposed restrictions on gender-related education and the exclusion of transgender students from participating in sports could have profound social and psychological effects on vulnerable students.

You might ask yourself, *Is it worth sacrificing educational equity and inclusivity in the name of local control and cultural conservatism?* The answer depends on whether you value short-term political gains or the long-term well-being of students from all walks of life. The policies outlined in *Project 2025* not only threaten to widen the achievement gap between rich and poor districts, but they also risk creating a more hostile and exclusionary school environment for LGBTQ+ students, exacerbating the mental health challenges these students already face.

You might wonder, *Is there a better path forward?* Instead of dismantling federal oversight and restricting discussions about gender identity, schools should focus on creating inclusive environments where all students—regardless of their background or identity—have the opportunity to succeed. Public education should be a too for lifting all students, not for perpetuating divisions and deepening inequalities. The choices we make today about education policy will shape the future for generations to come, and it's important to ensure that every student has the support and resources they need to thrive.

Chapter 7: The Role of the Courts and Law Enforcement

Imagine a future where federal agencies like the FBI and the Department of Justice (DOJ) are no longer viewed as independent enforcers of the law but as instruments of political agendas. Many people today perceive these institutions as biased, particularly in their high-profile investigations and prosecutions, leading to diminished public trust in the legal system. *Project 2025* seeks to address this perceived problem by "de-weaponizing" these agencies, proposing sweeping changes to their oversight and accountability.

But what does "de-weaponizing" actually mean? What are the potential consequences of increasing oversight of federal law enforcement agencies like the FBI and DOJ? And how will these changes impact public trust in these institutions? In this chapter, we'll explore *Project 2025's* proposals for the FBI and DOJ, discussing their potential effects on law enforcement operations, the legal system, and the relationship between government and the governed.

De-Weaponizing Federal Agencies

Project 2025 emphasizes the need to "de-weaponize" federal agencies like the FBI and DOJ. The term "weaponizing" refers to the belief that these agencies are being used as tools to advance political agendas, rather than serving as impartial enforcers of the law. In recent years, high-profile cases, such as the investigation into Russian interference in U.S. elections, the prosecution of political figures, and debates over the DOJ's role in addressing civil rights issues, have led to widespread accusations of bias.

You might be wondering, *What does it mean to "de-weaponize" these agencies?* At its core, this concept calls for reforms aimed at increasing oversight, ensuring greater accountability, and reducing the perception that these institutions are politically motivated. But there's more than meets the eye. Advocates of these reforms believe that the current structure of the FBI and DOJ gives too much discretionary power to individuals who can misuse their authority for political gain. **You might**

ask yourself, *Are these concerns valid?* While many see federal law enforcement agencies as critical to upholding the rule of law, others believe these institutions have become too politicized, especially in how they handle high-stakes investigations and legal proceedings.

Project 2025 proposes several mechanisms to increase oversight and accountability within the FBI and DOJ. These include:

- **Appointing politically neutral oversight boards** to review high-profile investigations.
- **Limiting the discretionary powers** of top officials within these agencies to ensure their decisions are based on legal precedents, rather than political considerations.
- **Requiring regular audits and reviews** of ongoing investigations to ensure transparency.
- **Implementing stricter regulations** for initiating investigations into political figures, reducing the risk of politically motivated probes.

You might be thinking, *Isn't more oversight a good thing?* After all, in a democracy, checks and balances are critical to preventing abuses of power. Ensuring that law enforcement agencies are transparent, accountable, and free from political influence should, in theory, build public trust and maintain the integrity of the legal system. However, the devil is in the details. **You might ask**, *How much oversight is too much?* While additional oversight can help guard against political bias, it can also lead to bureaucratic gridlock and slow down critical investigations especially if oversight bodies themselves are influenced by political concerns.

Increasing oversight of the FBI and DOJ, while well-intentioned, could have far-reaching consequences for how law enforcement operates. **You might be wondering**, *How will these changes affect investigations?* One potential outcome is that federal law enforcement agencies may become more hesitant to pursue high-profile cases, especially those involving political figures, out of fear of being perceived as biased. This could lead to a chilling effect, where important investigations are delayed, curtailed, or abandoned altogether.

Moreover, requiring greater oversight and review at multiple stages of an investigation could slow down the process significantly. **You might think**, *Shouldn't investigations be thorough anyway?* While thoroughness is crucial, adding too many layers of bureaucracy could make it more difficult for law enforcement to act swiftly, especially in cases where quick action is needed, such as national security threats or major criminal enterprises. **You might ask**, *What happens when law enforcement agencies are too slow to act?* In certain cases, delays can allow criminal activities to continue unchecked, potentially putting public safety at risk.

You might also wonder, *How does this impact national security?* The FBI, in particular, plays a central role in counterterrorism and national security investigations. Increasing oversight and limiting the discretionary powers of its leadership could complicate its ability to respond to fast-evolving threats, such as terrorism or cyberattacks. In cases where swift, decisive action is required, excessive bureaucracy could hamper the agency's effectiveness, ultimately endangering national security.

Public Trust in Legal Institutions

At the heart of *Project 2025*'s proposals is the belief that restoring public trust in federal law enforcement is critical. In recent years, trust in these institutions has eroded, with accusations from both sides of the political spectrum that the FBI and DOJ are either biased or politically motivated. **You might ask yourself**, *Why is trust in these institutions so important?* Public trust in law enforcement and the legal system is critical to maintaining the rule of law. When people believe that legal institutions are impartial and fair, they are more likely to accept the outcomes of investigations and prosecutions, even if those outcomes do not align with their personal beliefs or political preferences.

However, the challenge is that perceptions of bias are often rooted in broader political divisions. **You might wonder**, *Can increased oversight really restore trust?* While greater transparency and accountability can help address concerns about bias, it's unlikely that these reforms alone will fully restore trust in federal law enforcement agencies. In a highly polarized political environment, people are likely to view these agencies through the lens of their own political beliefs, making it difficult to achieve a consensus on whether an investigation or prosecution was conducted fairly.

Moreover, **you might think**, *What happens if oversight becomes too political?* There's a risk that creating new oversight bodies or increasing political scrutiny of the FBI and DOJ could itself become a source of bias. If these oversight mechanisms are staffed by politica appointees or subject to political pressures, they could end up exacerbating the very problems they were designed to solve. Instead of ensuring impartiality, these reforms could lead to further politicization of the legal system, making it even harder to rebuild public trust.

Balancing Accountability and Independence

You might be asking, *How do we strike the right balance between accountability and independence?* On the one hand, law enforcement agencies must be held accountable for their actions, especially in high-profile cases involving political figures. But on the other hand, these agencies must also be free to carry out their duties without undue political interference. Striking the right balance is essential to ensuring that law enforcement can operate effectively while maintaining public confidence.

Project 2025's proposals to increase FBI and DOJ oversight reflect a legitimate concern about the potential for political bias in law enforcement. However, **you might wonder**, *Is there a way to increase accountability without undermining the independence of these agencies?* One potential solution is to focus on internal reforms that promote transparency and accountability from within, rather than relying on external oversight bodies that may be influenced by political concerns. For example, creating stronger whistleblower protections, implementing regular internal audits, and promoting a culture of accountability within these agencies could help address concerns about bias without undermining their ability to function effectively.

Another approach might be to depoliticize the appointment process for key positions within the FBI and DOJ, ensuring that leaders are chosen based on their qualifications and experience rather than their political affiliations. **You might ask**, *Would this really make a difference?* While no system is perfect, reducing the influence of politics in these appointments could help restore public trust in the impartiality of law enforcement agencies, making them more accountable to the law and less beholden to political pressures.

Conclusion: The Future of Law Enforcement in America

As you consider the proposals laid out in *Project 2025*, it's important to weigh the potential benefits of increased oversight and accountability against the risks of over-politicization and bureaucratic gridlock. **You might ask yourself**, *Is it possible to de-weaponize federal law enforcement agencies without undermining their effectiveness?* The answer lies in finding the right balance between ensuring that these agencies are accountable to the public while preserving their independence from political influence.

Ultimately, the goal of any reform should be to strengthen public trust in the legal system, ensuring that all citizens—regardless of their political beliefs—feel confident that the FBI, DOJ, and other federal law enforcement agencies are acting in the best interests of justice. **You might wonder**, *How can we restore this trust?* The answer is not simple, but by promoting transparency, accountability, and impartiality within these institutions, we can begin to rebuild the public's faith in the rule of law.

As we move forward, it's essential to remain vigilant in guarding against both the politicization of law enforcement and the potential for abuse of power. Only by striking the right balance can we ensure that the legal institutions tasked with upholding justice continue to serve the interests of all Americans, rather than becoming tools of political agendas.

Chapter 8: Healthcare and Social Services

Imagine waking up one day to find that accessing healthcare depends not just on whether you need it but on whether you can afford it or meet new work requirements. That is the future that *Project 2025* envisions for the healthcare system in the United States: a system driven by privatization, deregulation, and personal responsibility rather than universal access and public support. This vision includes a push to deregulate the healthcare industry, reduce government involvement, and implement strict work requirements for Medicaid, the healthcare lifeline for millions of low-income Americans.

In this chapter, we will explore two of *Project 2025's* most significant healthcare and social services proposals: healthcare reform through deregulation and privatization, and the imposition of Medicaid work requirements. While these ideas are presented as solutions to inefficiencies and high costs in healthcare, they pose substantial risks to vulnerable populations, particularly low-income families, rural communities, and individuals who rely on Medicaid for essential services.

Healthcare Reform: Deregulation and Privatization

Project 2025 advocates for a healthcare system in which the government plays a minimal role, emphasizing deregulation and the expansion of private-sector solutions. Proponents argue that the free market, if left to its own devices, will naturally bring down healthcare costs through competition, innovation, and consumer choice. **You might think**, *Doesn't the free market usually lead to better services and lower prices?* That's often the case in industries where consumers have the time and ability to compare products and make informed decisions. But healthcare is different. It's a sector where patients don't get to choose when they get sick or injured, and most consumers lack the expertise to fully assess their treatment options.

Deregulation in the Healthcare System

Deregulation would involve rolling back many of the rules and guidelines that govern how healthcare providers operate and how insurance companies provide coverage. This could include removing requirements that insurers cover essential health benefits, such as mental health services, prescription drugs, maternity care, and pre-existing conditions. **You might ask yourself**, *Why are these regulations in place to begin with?* These rules were put into effect to protect consumers from being denied necessary care or charged exorbitant rates due to their medical histories. Without such protections, the healthcare landscape could shift dramatically, making it more difficult for people to obtain coverage for vital services.

You might be thinking, *Won't deregulation lead to cheaper options?* While deregulation might reduce costs for some, it could also cause the creation of "bare-bones" insurance plans that offer minimal coverage. For healthy people, these plans may seem an affordable option. But for those who develop chronic illnesses or need extensive medical care, they could find themselves saddled with crippling medical bills. Deregulation could also lead to a greater divide in healthcare access between those who can afford comprehensive plans and those who cannot.

Privatization of Healthcare

The privatization component of *Project 2025* suggests shifting more of the healthcare system to private companies, with the belief that the private sector can deliver more efficient and higher-quality services than government-run programs. **You might wonder**, *Why privatize healthcare?* Advocates of privatization argue that the private sector is more innovative and responsive to consumers' needs, unlike government bureaucracies, which they claim are slow, inefficient, and prone to waste.

However, privatizing health services can also have serious downsides. **You might ask**, *What happens when profit motives drive healthcare?* In a privatized system, healthcare providers and insurance companies are incentivized to prioritize profits over patients. This often leads to higher costs for care, as companies raise prices to maximize their earnings. In many cases, this could cause people being denied coverage for certain treatments or being forced to pay out of pocket for essential services.

You might be thinking, *Won't privatization improve efficiency and reduce costs overall?* While privatization can lead to innovation, it doesn't always lead to lower prices or better access for everyone. Instead, it can exacerbate inequalities in the healthcare system. Those with higher incomes can afford premium healthcare services, while low-income individuals are left with fewer options, less comprehensive coverage, and higher out-of-pocket costs.

Impact on Rural and Low-Income Communities

You might wonder, *How will deregulation and privatization affect rural and low-income communities?* Rural communities already face significant barriers to healthcare, including fewer healthcare providers, longer travel distances to reach hospitals or clinics, and higher rates of chronic illness. Deregulation could worsen these challenges. In many rural areas, the healthcare system is fragile, with hospitals and clinics already operating on thin margins. If federal regulations that protect access to care are rolled back, rural healthcare facilities may struggle to stay open.

In low-income communities, where access to affordable healthcare is already limited, privatization could further widen the gap between those who can afford quality care and those who cannot. **You might ask**, *Who benefits from privatization?* Privatization often benefits those with higher incomes who can afford to pay for private insurance and access top-tier healthcare services. For the millions of Americans who depend on Medicaid or other public programs, privatization could mean higher costs, fewer options, and more limited access to care.

Medicaid Work Requirements

Another key aspect of *Project 2025* is the imposition of work requirements for Medicaid recipients. Medicaid provides health coverage to over 75 million low-income individuals, including families, pregnant women, children, the elderly, and people with disabilities. For many, Medicaid is the only way they can afford healthcare. **You might be wondering**, *Why introduce work requirements for Medicaid?* Proponents of this policy argue that work requirements promote personal responsibility and reduce dependency on government assistance by encouraging individuals to find employment.

How Medicaid Work Requirements Operate

Under Medicaid work requirements, beneficiaries would need to meet certain employment or work-related criteria—such as holding a job, participating in job training, or volunteering in their community— to receive healthcare benefits. **You might think**, *That seems fair—shouldn't people work if they can?* While the idea of tying government benefits to employment might sound reasonable, the reality is far more complicated. Many Medicaid recipients already work, often in low-wage jobs that don't offer health insurance. These jobs can be unstable, seasonal, or part-time, making it difficult for workers to consistently meet the work requirements imposed by *Project 2025*.

Impact on Vulnerable Populations

You might ask, *What about people who can't work?* Many Medicaid recipients are unable to work due to illness, disability, or caregiving responsibilities. For example, an individual caring for an elderly parent or a child with special needs may not have the ability to work outside the home, but they still rely on Medicaid for essential healthcare services. Others may live in rural areas with limited job opportunities or face transportation challenges that make it difficult to maintain regular employment.

Medicaid work requirements could lead to hundreds of thousands of people losing their healthcare coverage, particularly those who are already struggling with barriers to employment. **You might wonder**, *How many people will lose coverage because of this?* Studies from states that have implemented work requirements show that many people lose coverage not because they refuse to work, but because they are unable to navigate the bureaucratic processes required to prove they meet the work requirements. This is particularly true for individuals with limited access to technology or who struggle with disabilities.

Losing Medicaid coverage can have devastating consequences for individuals and families. **You might ask**, *What happens when people lose access to healthcare?* Without Medicaid, many individuals will delay seeking medical care until their health problems become severe, leading to increased use of emergency rooms and higher healthcare costs in the long run. For individuals with chronic conditions such as diabetes, asthma, or heart disease, losing access to regular care and medications can cause life-threatening complications.

You might be thinking, *But won't exemptions protect people who are unable to work?* While some states offer exemptions for individuals who are unable to work due to disability or caregiving responsibilities, these exemptions can be difficult to obtain. The process of applying for and proving eligibility for an exemption is often confusing and time-consuming, particularly for those with limited education or access to resources. As a result, many people who are eligible for exemptions may still lose their coverage due to bureaucratic hurdles.

The Broader Implications for Public Health

The healthcare and social services reforms proposed by *Project 2025* would have wide-ranging implications not only for individual health but for public health as a whole. **You might wonder**, *How will these changes affect the overall healthcare system?* When large numbers of people lose access to healthcare, it doesn't just affect them—it places additional strain on hospitals, emergency rooms, and public health resources. Hospitals, particularly in rural areas, may see an influx of uninsured patients, which can strain already limited resources and lead to closures of vital healthcare facilities.

Moreover, **you might ask**, *What are the long-term costs of these reforms?* While *Project 2025* aims to reduce government spending on healthcare, the long-term costs of untreated illnesses, hospitalizations, and emergency care could far outweigh any short-term savings. As more people lose access to preventive care, chronic conditions are likely to worsen, leading to more expensive interventions down the road. In the end, the burden of these costs will fall on taxpayers, healthcare providers, and the broader healthcare system.

As you consider the healthcare reforms proposed by *Project 2025*, it's important to weigh the potential benefits of increased market competition and reduced government intervention against the risks of reduced access to care, higher costs, and a fragmented healthcare system. **You might ask yourself**, *Is privatization and deregulation the right path for healthcare reform?* While these policies may lower costs for some, they could also lead to significant disparities in access and quality of care, particularly for low-income and rural communities.

Medicaid work requirements, while intended to promote personal responsibility, could leave many of the most vulnerable without coverage, ultimately driving up healthcare costs and worsening health outcomes. **You might wonder**, *Is there a better way to reform healthcare?* A balanced approach that maintains protections for consumers, ensures access to affordable care for all, and supports vulnerable populations may be a more sustainable and equitable solution.

The choices made today about healthcare reform will shape the future of the healthcare system for generations to come. It's up to you to decide whether the vision outlined in *Project 2025* aligns with the values of access, equity, and care for all Americans.

Chapter 9: Impact on Democracy and Governance

Imagine living in a country where the balance of power, once central to its democratic integrity, starts to shift dramatically. The executive branch grows stronger, consolidating power and operating with less oversight, while federal programs that once supported civic engagement and ensured checks and balances are dismantled. This is the direction *Project 2025* could take American governance, fundamentally reshaping how democracy functions in the United States. You may ask yourself, *What will this mean for my role in society? How will my voice, my vote, and my participation in civic life be affected?*

In this chapter, we'll examine how *Project 2025's* focus on consolidating executive power and reducing federal oversight may challenge traditional checks and balances, and how these changes could have long-term effects on civic participation, voter turnout, and the way local governments operate. The potential consequences for democracy are far-reaching, and it's crucial to consider how these policies will alter not just governance but also the very foundation of civic life in America.

Executive Overreach and Governance

The heart of *Project 2025* is the consolidation of power within the executive branch. This strategy is based on the belief that the president should have more authority to direct the actions of federal agencies and that the bureaucracy should be streamlined to improve efficiency. **You might ask**, *Isn't efficiency in government a good thing?* In theory, yes. However, the concentration of power within the executive branch can lead to significant challenges for the democratic system of checks and balances that is designed to prevent any one branch of government from becoming too powerful.

The Role of Checks and Balances

The system of checks and balances, enshrined in the U.S. Constitution, ensures that no single branch of government—executive, legislative, or judicial—has unchecked power. Each branch has specific responsibilities and the ability to limit the actions of the other branches. For example, Congress makes the laws, but the president has the power to veto them. Similarly, the judiciary has the authority to interpret the Constitution and can overturn laws or executive actions that are deemed unconstitutional. **You might wonder**, *Why is this important?* Checks and balances are crucial because they maintain the separation of powers and ensure that no single entity can dominate the government or infringe on the rights of the people.

You might be thinking, *But doesn't the president need more power to get things done?* While it's true that presidents often face gridlock in Congress, which can slow down policy implementation, the consolidation of power in the executive branch poses risks to democracy. When the executive branch becomes too powerful, it can bypass or ignore the will of the legislature and the judiciary, weakening the foundational principles of governance.

How Project 2025 Threatens Checks and Balances

Project 2025 seeks to strengthen the executive branch by giving the president greater control over federal agencies and reducing the influence of independent bodies like the Department of Justice (DOJ), Environmental Protection Agency (EPA), and others. **You might ask**, *How does this affect checks and balances?* When the executive branch has greater control over agencies that are supposed to act independently, it can blur the line between impartial law enforcement and political influence. This could lead to scenarios where decisions about environmental protections, justice, or health regulations are made based on political motivations rather than what is best for the country.

For example, if the president gains more control over the DOJ, investigations into political allies or opponents might be influenced by personal or party interests rather than by impartial justice. **You might wonder**, *What does this mean for me?* It means that the law may no longer apply equally to everyone, leading to a loss of public trust in institutions that are supposed to protect citizens' rights and enforce the law fairly.

The weakening of checks and balances also threatens Congress's ability to serve as a counterweight to the executive branch. **You might ask,** *How does this impact my representation in government?* If the president can unilaterally bypass Congress, then your voice, represented by your elected officials, may be diminished. The legislative process exists to ensure that the interests of all Americans are considered before laws are passed or policies are implemented. By undermining the role of Congress, the executive branch could push through policies that are not in the best interest of the broader public, reducing democratic accountability.

Long-Term Effects on Civic Participation

In addition to concentrating power within the executive branch, *Project 2025* advocates for reducing federal oversight and control over certain programs, particularly those related to social services and education. These changes could have a profound impact on how engaged Americans are with their government and whether they feel empowered to participate in civic life.

Impact on Voter Turnout

One of the key ways that federal programs influence civic participation is by supporting initiatives that make voting more accessible, especially in underserved communities. Federal agencies often provide funding and resources to ensure that voter registration drives, education campaigns, and early voting options are available in all parts of the country. **You might be thinking,** *Isn't voting already accessible?* While some Americans may find it easy to vote, many others face significant barriers—such as long wait times, restricted voting hours, or lack of transportation to polling places.

If federal programs that support voting access are reduced or eliminated, it could disproportionately affect low-income communities, minorities, and rural areas. **You might ask yourself,** *How will this affect voter turnout?* With fewer resources to ensure accessible voting options, many eligible voters may be discouraged from participating in elections, particularly those who face systemic barriers to voting. This would likely lead to lower voter turnout, which undermines the legitimacy of election outcomes and reduces the overall health of democracy.

You might wonder, *Why does voter turnout matter?* High voter turnout is a sign of a vibrant democracy where citizens feel that their voices are heard and that their participation makes a difference. When voter turnout declines, it often reflects disillusionment or disengagement from the political process. In the long run, lower voter turnout can erode the legitimacy of elected officials and lead to policies that do not reflect the will of the people.

Effect on Civic Engagement

Beyond voting, federal programs play a crucial role in promoting civic engagement by supporting education, community development, and social services. **You might ask**, *How does the federal government encourage civic participation?* Programs like AmeriCorps and other public service initiatives are designed to engage young people and others in volunteerism, community projects, and local governance. These programs not only benefit communities but also promote a sense of civic responsibility and engagement among participants.

You might be thinking, *Why should the federal government fund civic engagement programs?* These programs help create a culture of participation, where citizens are encouraged to get involved in their communities and governance. When people participate in civic life—whether by volunteering, attending town hall meetings, or advocating for local issues—they are more likely to stay informed and engaged with the democratic process. **You might wonder**, *What happens if these programs are cut?* Reducing or eliminating federal support for civic engagement programs could lead to a decline in community involvement, particularly in underserved areas where local governments may lack the resources to provide similar opportunities.

State-Level Control and Local Governance

Project 2025 advocates for shifting many responsibilities from the federal government to the states, including control over education, healthcare, and social services. While this may seem like a move toward greater local autonomy, **you might ask**, *How does this impact democracy at the local level?* State governments often have less capacity than the federal government to administer large-scale programs, and the quality of services can vary dramatically from one state to another.

You might wonder, *What happens when states have more control over essential services?* In some cases, this could lead to more tailored solutions that reflect local needs. However, it also increases the risk of inequality between states. Wealthier states with more resources may be able to provide high-quality services, while poorer states may struggle to meet the needs of their citizens. This disparity could further erode trust in government, particularly in states where residents feel that they are not receiving adequate support or representation.

State-level control over programs also places more pressure on local governments to step in and fill gaps left by the federal government. **You might ask yourself**, *Are local governments equipped to handle this responsibility?* In many cases, local governments are underfunded and understaffed, making it difficult for them to manage additional responsibilities effectively. This could lead to lower quality services and increased frustration among residents, further reducing civic engagement and participation.

The Future of Democracy Under *Project 2025*

As you consider the implications of *Project 2025*, it's important to reflect on how these proposed changes to governance and democracy could affect not only the structure of government but also your role as a citizen. **You might ask yourself**, *What kind of democracy do I want to live in?* A democracy where power is concentrated in the hands of a few, or one where checks and balances ensure that all voices are heard?

The consolidation of power in the executive branch threatens the core principles of American democracy by undermining the system of checks and balances that has preserved freedom and equality for centuries. At the same time, reducing federal programs and shifting control to the states could lead to increased inequality, lower voter turnout, and less civic engagement—weakening the foundation of democracy itself.

You might wonder, *Is there a better way forward?* Strengthening democracy requires a commitment to ensuring that all citizens have access to the tools and resources they need to participate fully in civic life. Rather than concentrating power in the executive branch or reducing federal support for essential programs, efforts should focus on expanding access to voting, promoting civic education, and fostering greater engagement at the local level. Only by empowering all citizens to participate in governance can America's future remain strong and free.

Conclusion: The Future of America Under Project 2025

Imagine a future where the federal government has been radically reshaped, the balance of power shifts dramatically, and everyday life for millions of Americans is altered. This is the vision *Project 2025* presents—a blueprint for a conservative transformation that aims to al gn the federal government with deeply conservative values. But what does this mean for America's future? **You might be wondering**, *How will this affect my taxes, healthcare, education, and social services?* These policy shifts will undoubtedly impact every aspect of life in the United States, from the way we interact with government institutions to how we raise our children, care for our health, and participate in the economy.

In this conclusion, we will explore the prospects for future conservative governance under *Project 2025*, the tangible effects on the everyday lives of Americans, and what can be done by those who wish to resist or advocate for alternatives to these policies.

Prospects for Future Conservative Governance

Project 2025 envisions a future where conservative governance extends deep into the structures of federal institutions. At its core, the plan represents a dramatic shift away from decades of federal policy trends that emphasize regulation, social safety nets, and inclusivity. If a future conservative presidency embraces Project *2025*, the federal government could undergo a radical transformation. **You might ask**, *What would this transformation look like?* It would be characterized by deregulation, a reduction in the size of government, and an emphasis on individual responsibility and free-market principles.

Transforming Federal Institutions

One of the central goals of *Project 2025* is to reshape federal agencies by appointing individuals aligned with conservative values and scaling back the regulatory powers of agencies like the Environmental Protection Agency (EPA) and the Department of Justice (DOJ). **You might think**, *Why does it matter who runs these agencies?* These agencies play a crucial role in protecting public health, enforcing civil rights, and regulating industries to prevent abuses. By reducing their power and appointing leadership that may prioritize deregulation, environmental protections could be weakened, civil rights enforcement might slow, and corporate oversight could diminish.

Another key goal of *Project 2025* is to expand executive power, allowing the president to have more direct control over federal agencies and limit the checks and balances traditionally exercised by Congress and the courts. **You might wonder**, *How will this affect democracy?* By concentrating power in the hands of the executive, the potential for abuses of power grows, and the ability of Congress to represent the will of the people through legislative action may be diminished. This shift could weaken the democratic process, making the government less accountable to voters.

Policy Shifts and Conservative Values

At the policy level, *Project 2025* advocates for a return to conservative values in areas such as taxation, immigration, healthcare, and education. **You might ask**, *What are these values?* The policies outlined in the project emphasize limited government, free-market solutions, and traditional social values. This could mean lower taxes for corporations and high earners, stricter immigration enforcement, fewer federal social services, and the promotion of family values in education policy.

However, **you might be thinking**, *Does this benefit everyone?* While some individuals—particularly wealthy Americans and businesses—may benefit from lower taxes and reduced regulations, the broader population could face challenges. Reduced government programs might lead to less support for low-income individuals, children, the elderly, and those in need of healthcare or housing assistance.

The Everyday Impact on Americans

You might be asking yourself, *How will my life change under Project 2025?* The everyday impact of these policy shifts would be significant, affecting everything from how much you pay in taxes to the kind of healthcare you can access, the quality of your children's education, and the availability of social services in your community.

Taxes and Economic Policy

Under *Project 2025*, one of the primary changes would be a restructuring of the tax system. The plan calls for reducing corporate taxes and simplifying personal income tax brackets. **You might think**, *Lower taxes sound great, right?* In the short term, some individuals and businesses might benefit from lower tax rates, especially high earners and corporations. However, **you might wonder**, *How will the government pay for essential services?* Lower taxes could mean reduced revenue for programs like Medicaid, Social Security, and public education, shifting the burden of funding essential services to states or cutting them altogether.

You might be concerned, *How does this affect lower-income families?* The tax cuts proposed by *Project 2025* are likely to benefit wealthier Americans more than middle- and lower-income individuals. Additionally, by reducing the federal role in social services, these families might find themselves without the financial support they need for healthcare, childcare, and education.

Healthcare and Social Services

Project 2025 advocates privatizing health care and instituting Medicaid work requirements. **You might ask**, *What does this mean for access to healthcare?* The plan would likely cause reduced access to healthcare for millions of low-income Americans who rely on Medicaid. Work requirements could force individuals to choose between caring for a family member and maintaining healthcare coverage, while the privatization of healthcare could lead to higher costs and fewer protections for those with pre-existing conditions.

You might be wondering, *What happens if I lose my healthcare coverage?* Losing access to affordable healthcare could have devastating consequences for individuals with chronic illnesses or those who require ongoing medical care. Without federal protections, many might be forced to forgo necessary treatments, leading to poorer health outcomes and increased strain on emergency services.

Education and Civic Participation

In education, *Project 2025* seeks to reduce federal oversight and return control to states and local governments. **You might think**, *Doesn't local control make sense?* While local control can allow for policies that reflect community values, it can also lead to significant disparities between states. Wealthier states may have the resources to fund high-quality education, while poorer states might struggle to provide basic services. **You might wonder**, *How does this impact my child's education?* Reduced federal oversight could cause less equitable access to education, particularly for students from low-income families, minority groups, and rural communities.

Moreover, the emphasis on family values in education could lead to restrictions on teaching about gender, sexuality, and race. **You might be asking**, *How does this affect the broader culture?* Such restrictions could limit students' exposure to diverse perspectives and contribute to a more homogenized, less inclusive curriculum.

At the same time, *Project 2025*'s reduction of federal programs that promote civic participation—such as voter registration initiatives and education on voting rights—could lead to lower voter turnout, especially in communities that already face barriers to voting. **You might be thinking**, *How does this affect my role as a citizen?* With fewer resources dedicated to making voting accessible, individuals may feel less empowered to participate in the democratic process, weakening the very foundation of representative government.

What Can Be Done?

If the future described under *Project 2025* sounds concerning, **you might be asking**, *What can I do to resist or advocate for alternatives?* There are several ways to get involved and push back against the policies outlined in this plan.

Engage in Civic Participation

One of the most important things you can do is engage in the democratic process. **You might be thinking**, *But does my vote really matter?* Absolutely. Voting in local, state, and national elections is one of the most powerful tools you have to shape the direction of government. By staying informed and supporting candidates who advocate for policies that align with your values, you can influence the future of your community and country.

Beyond voting, **you might wonder**, *How can I stay engaged year-round?* Participating in town hall meetings, contacting your elected representatives, and joining grassroots organizations that work on issues you care about are all ways to stay involved in shaping policy. Civic participation doesn't end at the ballot box—it's an ongoing effort to hold your government accountable and ensure that your voice is heard.

Support Advocacy Groups

There are numerous advocacy groups and nonprofits that work to counter policies like those proposed in *Project 2025*. **You might ask,** *How can I get involved with these organizations?* You can support these groups by volunteering, donating, or simply spreading the word about their efforts. Organizations that focus on healthcare access, environmental protection, voting rights, and social justice are already working to challenge the policies proposed in *Project 2025* and offer alternative solutions.

You might be wondering, *What impact can these organizations have?* Advocacy groups play a crucial role in shaping public opinion, influencing legislation, and holding policy makers accountable. By supporting these organizations, you can amplify their efforts to protect civil rights, promote equity, and ensure that the government remains responsive to the needs of all Americans—not just the wealthy or powerful.

Advocate for Alternatives

Finally, if you're concerned about the direction *Project 2025* could take the country, you can advocate for alternative policies. **You might ask yourself**, *What policies would benefit everyone?* Alternatives could include proposals that expand access to healthcare, protect the environment, ensure equitable education, and promote voting rights. By advocating for policies that prioritize the well-being of all Americans, you can help build a future that reflects values of fairness, inclusivity, and justice.

Shaping the Future of America

As you reflect on the potential future under *Project 2025*, **you might be asking**, *What kind of country do I want to live in?* The policies outlined in this plan offer a vision of limited government, deregulation, and privatization—one that might benefit a select few but could leave many disadvantaged in the years to come…